Big Book of Loom Knit Cowls

LEISURE ARTS, INC. • Maumelle, Arkansas

EDITORIAL STAFF
Senior Product Director: Pam Stebbins
Creative Art Director: Katherine Laughlin
Technical Writer/Editor: Cathy Hardy
Associate Technical Editors: Linda A. Daley, Sarah J. Green, and Lois J. Long
Editorial Writer: Susan Frantz Wiles
Art Category Manager: Lora Puls
Graphic Artist: Cailen Cochran
Prepress Technician: Stephanie Johnson
Contributing Photography Stylist: Lori Wenger
Contributing Photographer: Jason Masters

BUSINESS STAFF
President and Chief Executive Officer: Fred F. Pruss
Senior Vice President of Operations: Jim Dittrich
Vice President of Retail Sales: Martha Adams
Chief Financial Officer: Tiffany P. Childers
Controller: Teresa Eby
Information Technology Director: Brian Roden
Director of E-Commerce: Mark Hawkins
Manager of E-Commerce: Robert Young

Library of Congress Control Number: 2015939794
ISBN-13/EAN: 978-1-4647-4048-0
UPC: 0-28906-06611-1

LOOK FOR THE CAMERA
in our instructions and
watch our technique
videos made just for you!
www.LeisureArts.com/6611

Whether your outfit is classic, sporty, romantic, or fun, there's a cowl design in this collection that you can loom knit to go with it! Kathy Norris has created 24 great designs for skill levels from Beginner to Intermediate, using a variety of yarns (from light weight to jumbo). You'll want them all!

Argyle

INTERMEDIATE

Finished Size: 5" wide x 26" circumference (12.75 cm x 66 cm)

SHOPPING LIST

Yarn (Medium Weight) MEDIUM 4
[3.5 ounces, 205 yards
(100 grams, 187 meters) per skein]:
- ☐ Main Color (Green) - 1 skein
- ☐ Contrasting Color (Dark Green) - 1 skein

Loom (straight, large gauge)
- ☐ 38 Pegs

Additional Supplies
- ☐ Knitting loom tool
- ☐ Crochet hook, size K (6.5 mm)
- ☐ Yarn needle

GAUGE INFORMATION

In pattern,
27 stitches = 5" (12.75 cm),
10 rows = 2" (5 cm)

FAIR ISLE KNITTING

In Fair Isle knitting, both Main Color (MC) and Contrasting Color (CC) are used in the same row. To change colors, bring the unused color between the pegs and to the inside of the loom. When you are ready to use that color again, place the yarn across the back with even tension and then underneath the strand you were using and to the front, ready to knit the next peg *(Fig. 2, page 57)*.

INSTRUCTIONS

This cowl is worked as flat knitting across the width. The ends will be sewn together to achieve the circumference.

Working on the **inside** of the loom from right to left, with MC, chain cast on 27 pegs *(Figs. 1a & b, page 57)*; work as flat knitting.

You may follow the written instructions or the chart on page 6 *(see Following A Chart, page 6)*.

Row 1: (K1, P1) 3 times, K2, with CC (leaving a long end to be woven in later) K5, with MC K1, with CC K5, with MC K2, (P1, K1) 3 times.

Row 2: K1, (P1, K1) 3 times, with CC K1, with MC K1, with CC K3, with MC K3, with CC K3, with MC K1, with CC K1, with MC K1, (P1, K1) 3 times.

Row 3: K1, (P1, K1) 3 times, with CC K2, with MC K1, with CC K1, with MC K5, with CC K1, with MC K1, with CC K2, with MC K1, (P1, K1) 3 times.

Row 4: K1, (P1, K1) 3 times, with CC K3, with MC K1, with CC K1, with MC K3, with CC K1, with MC K1, with CC K3, with MC K1, (P1, K1) 3 times.

Row 5: K1, (P1, K1) 3 times, with CC K2, with MC K3, with CC K1, with MC K1, with CC K1, with MC K3, with CC K2, with MC K1, (P1, K1) 3 times.

Row 6: K1, (P1, K1) 3 times, with CC K1, (with MC K5, with CC K1) twice, with MC K1, (P1, K1) 3 times.

Row 7: K1, (P1, K1) 3 times, with CC K2, with MC K3, with CC K1, with MC K1, with CC K1, with MC K3, with CC K2, with MC K1, (P1, K1) 3 times.

Row 8: K1, (P1, K1) 3 times, with CC K3, with MC K1, with CC K1, with MC K3, with CC K1, with MC K1, with CC K3, with MC K1, (P1, K1) 3 times.

Row 9: K1, (P1, K1) 3 times, with CC K2, with MC K1, with CC K1, with MC K5, with CC K1, with MC K1, with CC K2, with MC K1, (P1, K1) 3 times.

Row 10: K1, (P1, K1) 3 times, with CC K1, with MC K1, with CC K3, with MC K3, with CC K3, with MC K1, with CC K1, with MC K1, (P1, K1) 3 times.

Repeat Rows 1-10 for pattern until piece measures approximately 26" (66 cm) from cast on edge, ending by working Row 10.

Cut CC; using MC, work chain one bind off across *(Figs. 6a-c, page 60)* leaving a long end for sewing.

Weave bound off and cast on stitches together *(Figs. 8b & c, page 61)*.

CHART

Row																												Row
10		—		—		—		■		■	■	■				■	■	■		■		—		—		—		
		—		—		—		■	■		■						■		■	■		—		—		—		9
8		—		—		—		■	■	■		■				■		■	■	■		—		—		—		
		—		—		—		■	■				■		■				■	■		—		—		—		7
6		—		—		—		■						■						■		—		—		—		
		—		—		—		■	■				■		■				■	■		—		—		—		5
4		—		—		—		■	■	■		■				■		■	■	■		—		—		—		
		—		—		—		■	■		■						■		■	■		—		—		—		3
2		—		—		—		■		■	■	■				■	■	■		■		—		—		—		
		—		—		—			■	■	■	■	■		■	■	■	■	■			—		—		—		1

KEY

☐ - knit using Main Color

— - purl using Main Color

■ - knit using Contrasting Color

FOLLOWING A CHART

The chart shows each stitch as a square indicating what color and stitch it should be. Follow the chart in the same direction that you are working the row. You can use a ruler or sticky notes to keep your place.

Bandana

 EASY

Shown on page 9.

Finished Size: 13" high x 27" circumference (33 cm x 68.5 cm)

SHOPPING LIST

Yarn (Light Weight) LIGHT 3
[1.75 ounces, 125 yards
(50 grams, 114 meters) per skein]:
- ☐ 2 skeins

Loom (small gauge)
- ☐ 96 Pegs (minimum)

Additional Supplies
- ☐ Knitting loom tool
- ☐ Crochet hook, size H (5 mm)
- ☐ Yarn needle

GAUGE INFORMATION

In Twisted Stockinette Stitch (e-wrap knit every row),
14 stitches and 24 rows = 4" (10 cm)

TECHNIQUES USED

- Left e-wrap decrease *(Fig. 4c, page 59)*
- Right e-wrap decrease *(Fig. 4f, page 59)*
- Left purl decrease *(Figs. 5a-c, page 59)*
- Right purl decrease *(Figs. 5d-f, page 59)*

INSTRUCTIONS

Working on the **inside** of the loom from right to left, chain cast on 96 pegs *(Figs. 1a & b, page 57)*; work as flat knitting.

Row 1: Purl across.

Row 2: E-wrap knit across.

Row 3: Purl across.

Rows 4-9: Repeat Rows 2 and 3, 3 times.

Rows 10-19: E-wrap knit across.

Row 20: P 25, EWK 46, P 25.

Row 21: E-wrap knit across.

Rows 22-25: Repeat Rows 20 and 21 twice.

Row 26: Bind off 21 pegs using chain one bind off *(Figs. 6a & b, page 60)* and place loop from hook onto next empty peg, P4, EWK 46, P5; bind off last 20 pegs using chain one bind off, cut yarn leaving a long end for sewing and pull end through loop *(Fig. 6c, page 60)*: 56 pegs remaining.

SHAPING

Row 1: Working from right to left, place a slip knot on an empty peg to temporarily hold the yarn in place; e-wrap knit across; remove slip knot.

When decreasing, move the end stitches so that there are no skipped pegs.

Row 2: P5, left e-wrap decrease, e-wrap knit across to last 7 pegs, right e-wrap decrease, P5: 54 pegs remaining.

Row 3: E-wrap knit across.

Rows 4-43: Repeat Rows 2 and 3, 20 times: 14 pegs remaining.

Row 44: P5, left e-wrap decrease, right e-wrap decrease, P5: 12 pegs remaining.

Row 45: E-wrap knit across.

Row 46: P4, left purl decrease, right purl decrease, P4: 10 pegs remaining.

Row 47: E-wrap knit across.

Row 48: P3, left purl decrease, right purl decrease, P3: 8 pegs remaining.

Row 49: E-wrap knit across.

Row 50: P2, left purl decrease, right purl decrease, P2: 6 pegs remaining.

Row 51: E-wrap knit across.

Row 52: P1, left purl decrease, right purl decrease, P1: 4 pegs remaining.

Row 53: E-wrap knit across.

Row 54: Left purl decrease, right purl decrease: 2 pegs remaining.

Row 55: EWK2.

Row 56: Left purl decrease; cut yarn and pull yarn end through loop.

Weave end of rows together from cast on edge to Shaping *(Fig. 8a, page 61)*.

Beehive

 **BEGINNER**

Finished Size: 5¾" high x 29½" circumference (14.5 cm x 75 cm)

SHOPPING LIST

Yarn (Medium Weight) MEDIUM 4
[5 ounces, 256 yards
(141 grams, 234 meters) per skein]:
- ☐ 1 skein

Loom (straight, large gauge)
- ☐ 50 Pegs

Additional Supplies
- ☐ Knitting loom tool
- ☐ Crochet hook, size K (6.5 mm)
- ☐ Yarn needle

GAUGE INFORMATION

In Stockinette Stitch (knit every row),
13 stitches = 4" (10 cm)
In pattern, 16 rows = 1½" (3.75 cm) unstretched

INSTRUCTIONS

This cowl is worked in two flat panels which are sewn together to achieve the circumference.

PANEL (Make 2)

Working on the **inside** of the loom from right to left, chain cast on all 50 pegs *(Figs. 1a & b, page 57)*; work as flat knitting.

Rows 1-4: Purl across.

Rows 5-8: Knit across.

Rows 9-60: Repeat Rows 1-8, 6 times; then repeat Rows 1-4 once **more**.

Work chain one bind off across *(Figs. 6a-c, page 60)* leaving a long end for sewing.

Matching bound off edges of Panels, weave end of rows together on each end to form the cowl *(Fig. 8a, page 61)*.

Brioche

EASY

Finished Size: 5½" high x 24" circumference (14 cm x 61 cm)

SHOPPING LIST

Yarn (Medium Weight) 
[5 ounces, 251 yards
(142 grams, 230 meters) per skein]:
- ☐ 1 skein

Loom (straight, large gauge)
- ☐ 50 Pegs

Additional Supplies
- ☐ Knitting loom tool
- ☐ Crochet hook, size K (6.5 mm)
- ☐ Yarn needle

GAUGE INFORMATION

In brioche pattern, 20 stitches = 5½" (14 cm)

INSTRUCTIONS

This cowl is worked as flat knitting across the height. The ends will be sewn together to achieve the circumference.

Working on the **inside** of the loom from right to left, chain cast on 20 pegs *(Figs. 1a & b, page 57)*; work as flat knitting.

Rows 1 and 2: Knit across.

Row 3: Skip 1 with yarn in **front** by placing a strand of yarn in **front** of the first peg and above the existing loop, knit the next peg, ★ skip 1 with yarn in **front**, K1 *(Fig. A)*; repeat from ★ across. There will be 2 strands in front of each skipped peg.

Fig. A

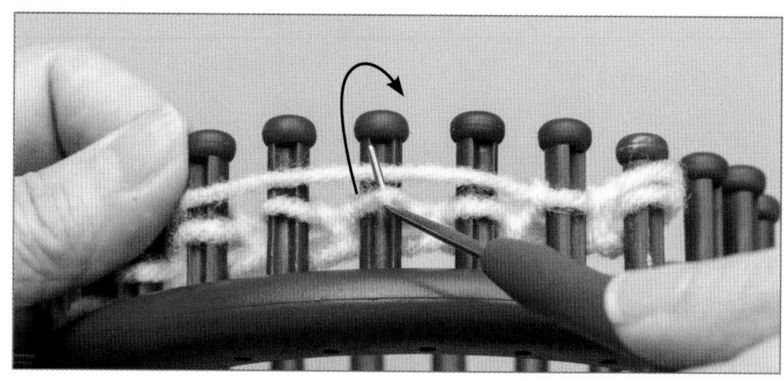

Row 4: ★ Skip 1 with yarn in **front**, P1 treating the 2 strands as one *(Fig. B)*; repeat from ★ across.

Fig. B

Row 5: ★ Skip 1 with yarn in **front**, K1; repeat from ★ across.

Row 6: ★ Skip 1 with yarn in **front**, P1; repeat from ★ across.

Repeat Rows 5 and 6 for brioche pattern until piece measures approximately 23½" (59.5 cm) from cast on edge, ending by working Row 5.

Next Row: (K1, P1) across.

Last 2 Rows: Knit across.

Work chain one bind off across *(Figs. 6a-c, page 60)* leaving a long end for sewing.

Weave bound off and cast on stitches together *(Figs. 8b & c, page 61)*, then weave through center of seam and gather to measure approximately 3" (7.5 cm); secure yarn.

Broken Cables

INTERMEDIATE

Finished Size: 6" high x 28" circumference (15 cm x 71 cm)

SHOPPING LIST

Yarn (Bulky Weight) BULKY 5
[12.7 ounces, 448 yards
(360 grams, 410 meters) per skein]:
- ☐ 1 skein

Loom (straight, large gauge)
- ☐ 50 Pegs

Additional Supplies
- ☐ Knitting loom tool
- ☐ Crochet hook, size K (6.5 mm)
- ☐ Cable needle
- ☐ Yarn needle

GAUGE INFORMATION

In pattern,
10 stitches = 3½" (9 cm),
8 rows = 2" (5 cm)

STITCH GUIDE

CABLE (uses next 4 pegs)

This cable is worked on a **right** to **left** row and leans to the right. Place the stitches from the next 2 pegs (pegs A & B) onto a cable needle and let it hang at the inside of the loom. Bring the working yarn behind the 2 empty pegs and to the outside of the loom *(Fig. A)*.

Fig. A

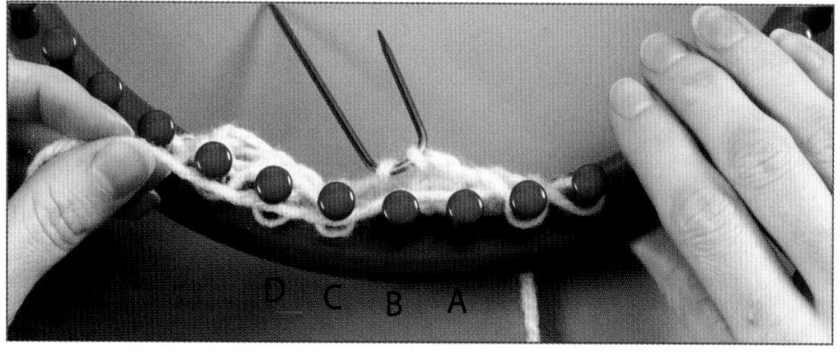

Knit the next 2 pegs (pegs C & D), then use the tool to move them to the empty pegs, keeping them in the same order *(Fig. B)*.

Fig. B

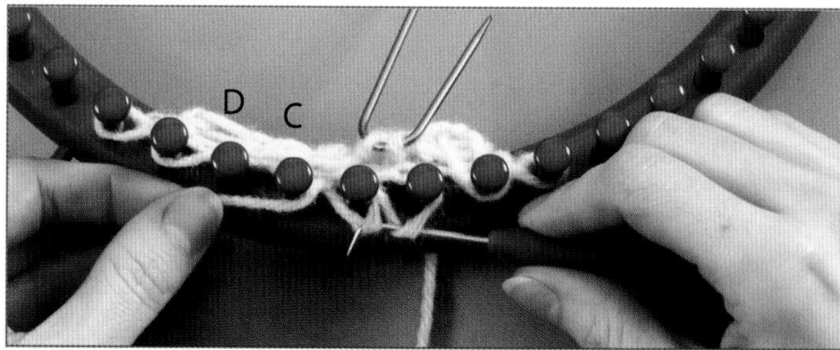

With the working yarn outside the loom, place the stitches from the cable needle onto the newly vacated pegs, keeping them in the same order, and knit them. Tighten the stitches to prevent elongated stitches.

TIP The stitches should always be worked **loosely**, allowing them to be easily moved.

INSTRUCTIONS

This cowl is worked in two flat panels which are sewn together to achieve the circumference.

PANEL (Make 2)

Working on the **inside** of the loom from right to left, chain cast on 42 pegs *(Figs. 1a & b, page 57)*; work as flat knitting.

Row 1: K1, P1, K4, (P6, K4) 3 times, P5, K1.

Row 2: K1, P5, K4, (P6, K4) 3 times, P1, K1.

Rows 3 and 4: Repeat Rows 1 and 2.

Row 5: K1, P1, work Cable, (P6, work Cable) 3 times, P5, K1.

Row 6: K1, P5, K4, (P6, K4) 3 times, P1, K1.

Rows 7 and 8: Repeat Rows 1 and 2.

Row 9: K1, P6, (K4, P6) 3 times, K5.

Row 10: K5, P6, (K4, P6) 3 times, K1.

Rows 11 and 12: Repeat Rows 9 and 10.

Row 13: K1, (P6, work Cable) 4 times, K1.

Row 14: K5, P6, (K4, P6) 3 times, K1.

Rows 15 and 16: Repeat Rows 9 and 10.

Rows 17-23: Repeat Rows 1-7.

Work sewn bind off across *(Figs. 7a & b, page 60)* leaving a long end for sewing.

Matching bound off edges of Panels, weave end of rows together on each end to form the cowl *(Fig. 8a, page 61)*.

Cable Look-a-Like

INTERMEDIATE

Finished Size: 7" high x 26" circumference (17.75 cm x 66 cm)

SHOPPING LIST

Yarn (Super Bulky Weight) 

[6 ounces, 106 yards
(170 grams, 97 meters) per skein]:

- ☐ 1 skein

Loom (round, large gauge)

- ☐ 24 Pegs

Additional Supplies

- ☐ Knitting loom tool
- ☐ Crochet hook, size K (6.5 mm)
- ☐ Yarn needle

GAUGE INFORMATION

In pattern,
22 stitches = 7" (17.75 cm),
10 rows = 3¼" (8.25 cm)

TECHNIQUE USED

Left decrease *(Figs. 4a & b, page 58)*

The cable look is achieved with decreases instead of using a cable needle.

INSTRUCTIONS

This cowl is worked as flat knitting across the width. The ends will be sewn together to form the circumference.

Working on the **inside** of the loom from right to left, chain cast on 22 pegs *(Figs. 1a & b, page 57)*; work as flat knitting.

Rows 1-4: K1, (P1, K1) twice, P3, K6, P3, K1, (P1, K1) twice.

Row 5: K1, (P1, K1) twice, P3, K2, left decrease, move the loop just made to the empty peg, (move loop on next peg to empty peg and knit it) twice, e-wrap next peg (counter-clockwise without knitting it), P3, K1, (P1, K1) twice.

Row 6: K1, (P1, K1) twice, P3, EWK1 (clockwise), K5, P3, K1, (P1, K1) twice.

Row 7: K1, (P1, K1) twice, P3, K1, left decrease, move the loop just made to the empty peg, (move loop on next peg to empty peg and knit it) twice, e-wrap next peg (counter-clockwise without knitting it), K1, P3, K1, (P1, K1) twice.

Row 8: K1, (P1, K1) twice, P3, K1, EWK1 (clockwise), K4, P3, K1, (P1, K1) twice.

Row 9: K1, (P1, K1) twice, P3, left decrease, move the loop just made to the empty peg, (move loop on next peg to empty peg and knit it) twice, e-wrap next peg (counter-clockwise without knitting it), K2, P3, K1, (P1, K1) twice.

Row 10: K1, (P1, K1) twice, P3, K2, EWK1 (clockwise), K3, P3, K1, (P1, K1) twice.

Rows 11-80: Repeat Rows 1-10, 7 times.

Work chain one bind off across *(Figs. 6a-c, page 60)* leaving a long end for sewing.

Weave bound off and cast on stitches together *(Figs. 8b & c, page 61)*.

Collared Lace

INTERMEDIATE

Finished Size: 7" high x 28" circumference (17.75 cm x 71 cm)

SHOPPING LIST

Yarn (Medium Weight) MEDIUM 4
[3.5 ounces, 208 yards
(100 grams, 190 meters) per skein]:
- ☐ 1 skein

Loom (straight, large gauge)
- ☐ 50 Pegs

Additional Supplies
- ☐ Knitting loom tool
- ☐ Crochet hook, size K (6.5 mm)
- ☐ Yarn needle
- ☐ Sewing needle and matching thread (optional)

GAUGE INFORMATION

In Garter Stitch (knit 1 row, purl 1 row),
16 stitches = 4½" (11.5 cm)
In lace pattern,
24 stitches = 7" (17.75 cm)

TECHNIQUES USED

- Left decrease *(Figs. 4a & b, page 58)*
- Right purl decrease *(Figs. 5d-f, page 59)*

STITCH GUIDE

To skip 1 with yarn in back at the beginning of a row creates a finished look to the vertical edge. Place the working yarn **behind** the peg to be skipped.

To skip 1 with yarn in front before a decrease creates a hole. Move the loop from the peg to be skipped to the next peg, with yarn in **front** of the skipped peg, complete the decrease.

To work short rows, wrap the peg indicated *(Figs. 3a & b, page 58)*, then reverse the direction you are working, leaving the remaining 24 pegs for the Cowl unworked.

To knit a wrapped peg, knit the peg by lifting both loops over the top strand and off the peg.

INSTRUCTIONS

Beginning at the center back, the Cowl is worked in a lace pattern and the Collar is worked in Garter Stitch using short rows worked across the Collar only so that the Collar has twice as many rows as the Cowl.

COLLAR & COWL - First Side

Working on the **inside** of the loom from right to left, chain cast on 40 pegs *(Figs. 1a & b, page 57)*; work as flat knitting.

Row 1: Skip 1 with yarn in **back**, K 15, wrap next peg.

Row 2: P 15, K1.

Row 3: Skip 1 with yarn in **back**, K 16, skip 1 with yarn in **front**, left decrease, ★ K1, skip 1 with yarn in **front**, left decrease; repeat from ★ across.

Row 4: (P1, skip 1 with yarn in **front**, right purl decrease) 8 times, P 15, K1.

Repeat Rows 1-4 for pattern until Cowl measures approximately 7" (18 cm) from cast on edge, ending by working Row 4. The Collar will be longer than the Cowl.

Work chain one bind off across 17 pegs (Collar) *(Figs. 6a & b, page 60)*, placing loop from hook onto next empty peg: 24 pegs remaining.

COWL

Row 1: (K1, skip 1 with yarn in **front**, left decrease) across.

Row 2: (P1, skip 1 with yarn in **front**, right purl decrease) across.

Repeat Rows 1 and 2 for pattern until Cowl measures approximately 14" (35.5 cm) from bound off edge, ending by working Row 2.

COLLAR & COWL - Second Side

Chain cast on 16 pegs for Collar: 40 pegs.

Repeat Rows 1-4 of First Side for pattern until Second Side measures same as First Side, ending by working Row 4.

Work chain one bind off across *(Fig. 6c, page 60)* leaving a long end for sewing.

Sew bound off and cast on sts together across Cowl, then sew across the Collar, making sure the seam won't show when Collar is folded over.

Optional: With sewing needle and matching thread, tack Collar to Cowl at seam.

Double Ruffle

EASY

Finished Size: 8" high x 23" circumference (20.5 cm x 58.5 cm)

SHOPPING LIST

Yarn (Medium Weight) MEDIUM 4
[2.8 ounces, 160 yards
(80 grams, 146 meters) per skein]:
☐ Purple - 1 skein
(Super Bulky Weight, Ruffle yarn) SUPER BULKY 6
[1.41 ounces, 24 yards
(40 grams, 22 meters) per hank]:
☐ 1 hank

Loom (round, large gauge)
☐ 24 Pegs

Additional Supplies
☐ Knitting loom tool
☐ Crochet hook, size K (6.5 mm)
☐ Yarn needle

This cowl is worked holding two strands of Purple together as one throughout. Roll the yarn into two balls or pull one strand from the center and one from the outside of the skein.

A separate strand of Ruffle yarn is used at each side edge of cowl. Roll the Ruffle yarn into two balls.

GAUGE INFORMATION

In Twisted Stockinette Stitch (e-wrap knit every row), holding 2 strands of Purple together,
17 stitches = 6" (15.25 cm) excluding ruffles,
14 rows = 4" (10 cm)

INSTRUCTIONS

This cowl is worked as flat knitting across the width. The ends will be sewn together to form the circumference.

Work the cast on as follows: Bring end of Ruffle yarn up through the center of the loom and place the first loop on the first peg. Holding 2 strands of Purple together as one, e-wrap knit the same peg (bringing the Ruffle yarn over the loop). Using Purple, e-wrap 15 pegs. Bring end of second ball of Ruffle yarn up through the center of the loom and place the first loop on the next peg. Using Purple, e-wrap knit the same peg: 17 pegs.

Row 1: Holding the Ruffle yarn at the inside of the loom, place the next loop of Ruffle yarn on first peg, bring the bottom loop over the top loop; place the next loop of second ball of Ruffle yarn on last peg, bring the bottom loop over the top loop. Using Purple, e-wrap knit all 17 pegs.

Repeat Row 1 for pattern until piece measures approximately 23" (58.5 cm) from cast on edge, ending with working yarn on the right-hand edge.

Work chain one bind off across *(Figs. 6a-c, page 60)* leaving a long end for sewing.

Cut Ruffle yarn close to work.

Weave bound off and cast on stitches together *(Figs. 8b & c, page 61)*. It is not necessary to sew Ruffle yarn together.

Mobius

BEGINNER

Finished Size: 8½" high x 34" circumference (21.5 cm x 86.5 cm)

SHOPPING LIST

Yarn (Medium Weight) MEDIUM 4
[3.5 ounces, 151 yards
(100 grams, 138 meters) per skein]:
- ☐ 2 skeins

Loom (round, large gauge)
- ☐ 36 Pegs

Additional Supplies
- ☐ Knitting loom tool
- ☐ Crochet hook, size K (6.5 mm)
- ☐ Yarn needle

GAUGE INFORMATION

In Garter Stitch (knit 1 row, purl 1 row),
14 stitches and 28 rows = 4" (10 cm)

INSTRUCTIONS

This cowl is worked as flat knitting across the width. The ends will be sewn together to achieve the circumference.

Working on the **inside** of the loom from right to left, chain cast on 30 pegs *(Figs. 1a & b, page 57)*; work as flat knitting.

Row 1: Knit across.

Row 2: Purl across.

Repeat Rows 1 and 2 for Garter Stitch until piece measures approximately 34" (86.5 cm) from cast on edge, ending by working Row 2.

Work chain one bind off across *(Figs. 6a-c, page 60)*.

Twist piece once and weave bound off and cast on stitches together to form the mobius *(Figs. 8b & c, page 61)*.

Filigree

EASY

Finished Size: 6" high x 24¾" circumference (15 cm x 63 cm)

SHOPPING LIST

Yarn (Bulky Weight) BULKY 5
[3.5 ounces, 109 yards
(100 grams, 100 meters) per skein]:

- ☐ White - 1 skein
- ☐ Black - 1 skein

Loom (straight, large gauge)

- ☐ 62 Pegs

Additional Supplies

- ☐ Knitting loom tool
- ☐ Crochet hook, size K (6.5 mm)

GAUGE INFORMATION

In pattern, 10 stitches = 4" (10 cm)

CHANGING COLORS

When changing colors, do **not** cut the yarn; drop the color that you are working with to the inside of the loom. Then pick up the next color from underneath the strand *(Fig. 2, page 57)*.

INSTRUCTIONS

Working on the **inside** of the loom from right to left and using White, chain cast on all 62 pegs *(Figs. 1a & b, page 57)*; work as circular knitting.

Skipping a peg combines two colors to form a pattern that looks like you changed colors every other stitch. Only one color is used on each round, alternating the colors every two rounds.

To skip 1, bring the working yarn to the inside of the loom and **behind** the peg to be skipped. Move the working yarn to the front to work the next stitch. The strand will **not** show on the **right** side.

Rnd 1: With White, knit around.

Rnd 2: Purl around.

Rnd 3: With Black, (K1, skip 1) around.

Rnd 4: (P1, skip 1) around.

Rnd 5: With White, knit around.

Rnd 6: Purl around.

Rnd 7: With Black, (skip 1, K1) around.

Rnd 8: (Skip 1, P1) around.

Repeat Rnds 1-8 for pattern until piece measures approximately 6" (15 cm) from cast on edge, ending by working Rnd 2; cut Black.

Work chain one bind off around *(Figs. 6a-c, page 60)*.

Gathers

EASY

Finished Size: 18½" high x 45" circumference (47 cm x 114.5 cm)

SHOPPING LIST

Yarn (Bulky Weight) BULKY 5
[3 ounces, 144 yards
(85 grams, 132 meters) per skein]:
- ☐ 3 skeins

Loom (round, extra large gauge)
- ☐ 40 or 41 Pegs

Additional Supplies
- ☐ Knitting loom tool
- ☐ Crochet hook, size K (6.5 mm)
- ☐ Yarn needle

GAUGE INFORMATION

In Twisted Stockinette Stitch (e-wrap every row),
8 stitches = 3¾" (9.5 cm)

TECHNIQUE USED

Right e-wrap decrease *(Fig. 4f, page 59)*

INSTRUCTIONS

This cowl is worked as flat knitting across the width. The ends will be sewn together to achieve the circumference. Eyelets are made along the right hand edge. The I-Cord Tie will be woven through these spaces to gather the top edge of the cowl.

BODY

Working on the **inside** of the loom from right to left, chain cast on 40 pegs *(Figs. 1a & b, page 57)*; work as flat knitting.

Row 1: E-wrap knit across to last 3 pegs, P1, EWK1, P1.

Row 2 (Eyelet row)**:** P1, EWK1, P1, e-wrap knit across to last 5 pegs, right e-wrap decrease, move loop just made to empty peg, skip 1 with yarn in **front**, EWK3.

Row 3: P3, e-wrap knit across to last 3 pegs, P1, EWK1, P1.

Row 4: P1, EWK1, P1, e-wrap knit across to last 3 pegs, P3.

Row 5: E-wrap knit across to last 3 pegs, P1, EWK1, P1.

Row 6: P1, EWK1, P1, e-wrap knit across.

Row 7: P3, e-wrap knit across to last 3 pegs, P1, EWK1, P1.

Row 8: P1, EWK1, P1, e-wrap knit across to last 3 pegs, P3.

Repeat Rows 1-8 for pattern until piece measures approximately 45" (114.5 cm) from cast on edge, ending by working Row 8.

Work chain one bind off across *(Figs. 6a-c, page 60)* leaving a long end for sewing.

Weave bound off and cast on stitches together *(Figs. 8b & c, page 61)*.

I-CORD TIE

E-wrap cast on 4 pegs from left to right.

E-wrap knit one row.

Work I-Cord as follows:

★ Bring the working yarn across the inside of the loom, then outside to the left of the first peg that was worked *(Fig. A)*. Working counter-clockwise, e-wrap knit the 4 pegs; repeat from ★ until I-cord measures approximately 55" (139.5 cm), giving the cord a tug every few rounds to close the gap between the first and last stitches *(Fig. B)*.

Fig. A

Fig. B

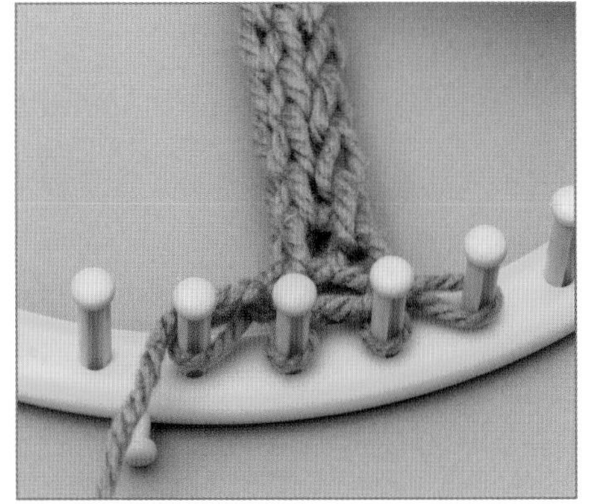

Cut yarn leaving a long end for sewing. Thread yarn needle with end and insert the yarn needle in the each loop from bottom to top, lifting each loop off the peg and onto the yarn end, gather stitches and secure end.

Lay the cowl flat with the seam at one side. Beginning at the fold, weave the Tie through the eyelets; tie in a bow.

Hooded Cowl

EASY

Finished Size: 15" high at Hood x 34" circumference (38 cm x 86.5 cm)

SHOPPING LIST

Yarn (Super Bulky Weight) 
[3.5 ounces, 108 yards
(100 grams, 99 meters) per skein]:

- ☐ 2 skeins

Loom (round, extra large gauge)

- ☐ 36 Pegs

Additional Supplies

- ☐ Knitting loom tool
- ☐ Crochet hook, size K (6.5 mm)
- ☐ Yarn needle

GAUGE INFORMATION

In Twisted Stockinette Stitch (e-wrap knit every row),
8 stitches = 3¾" (9.5 cm)

STITCH GUIDE

To skip 1 at the beginning of a row creates a finished look to the vertical edge. Place the working yarn **behind** the peg to be skipped.

To work short rows, wrap the peg indicated *(Figs. 3a & b, page 58)*, then reverse the direction you are working, leaving the remaining pegs unworked.

To e-wrap knit a wrapped peg, e-wrap knit the peg by lifting both loops over the top loop and off the peg.

INSTRUCTIONS

This piece is worked as flat knitting across the width of the cowl and the height of the hood. The ends of the cowl will be sewn together to achieve the circumference and the hood will be seamed across the top edge.

Beginning at the center front of the cowl, short rows are used to form the shaping. Stitches will be added on for the hood, then bound off to finish the cowl.

COWL - First Side

Working on the **inside** of the loom from right to left, chain cast on 12 pegs *(Figs. 1a & b, page 57)*; work as flat knitting.

Row 1: Skip 1, P1, EWK1, P1, EWK8.

Row 2: Skip 1, e-wrap knit across.

Row 3: Skip 1, P1, EWK1, P1, EWK4, wrap next peg, leave remaining 4 pegs unworked.

Row 4: E-wrap knit across.

Rows 5-32: Repeat Rows 1-4, 7 times.

Row 33: Skip 1, P1, EWK1, P1, EWK8, chain cast on 22 pegs for hood working on outside of loom *(Fig. 1c, page 57)*: 34 pegs.

HOOD

Row 1: E-wrap knit across.

Row 2: Skip 1, P1, EWK1, P1, EWK8, P 22.

Rows 3 and 4: Repeat Rows 1 and 2.

Row 5: E-wrap knit across.

Row 6: Skip 1, P1, EWK1, P1, e-wrap knit across.

Repeat Rows 5 and 6 for pattern until Hood measures approximately 16" (40.5 cm) from cast on edge of Hood, ending by working Row 6.

Repeat Rows 1 and 2 twice.

COWL - Second Side

Row 1: Work chain one bind off across *(Figs. 6a-c, page 60)* 23 pegs and place loop on hook onto next empty peg; e-wrap knit across: 12 pegs remaining.

Rows 2-33: Repeat Rows 1-4 of First Side, 8 times.

Work chain one bind off across leaving a long end for sewing.

Weave bound off and cast on stitches of Cowl together to form a circle *(Figs. 8b & c, page 61)*.

Fold Hood in half and weave end of rows together to form top seam *(Fig. 8a, page 61)*.

Houndstooth

INTERMEDIATE

Finished Size: 6" high x 21" circumference (15 cm x 53.5 cm)

SHOPPING LIST

Yarn (Medium Weight) MEDIUM 4
[5 ounces, 251 yards
(142 grams, 230 meters) per skein]:
- ☐ Main Color (Black) - 1 skein
- ☐ Contrasting Color (Grey) - 1 skein

Loom (round, large gauge)
- ☐ 30 Pegs

Additional Supplies
- ☐ Knitting loom tool
- ☐ Crochet hook, size K (6.5 mm)
- ☐ Yarn needle

GAUGE INFORMATION

In pattern, 28 stitches = 6" (15 cm)

FAIR ISLE KNITTING

In Fair Isle knitting, both Main Color (MC) and Contrasting Color (CC) are used in the same row. To change colors, bring the unused color between the pegs and to the inside of the loom. When you are ready to use that color again, place the yarn across the back with even tension and then underneath the strand you were using and to the front, ready to knit the next peg *(Fig. 2, page 57)*.

INSTRUCTIONS

This cowl is worked as flat knitting across the width. The ends will be sewn together to achieve the circumference.

Working on the **inside** of the loom from right to left and using MC, chain cast on 28 pegs *(Figs. 1a & b, page 57)*; work as flat knitting.

To skip 1 with yarn in back at the beginning of a row creates a finished look to the vertical edge. Place the working yarn **behind** the peg to be skipped.

Row 1: Skip 1, K5, with CC K1, ★ with MC K3, with CC K1; repeat from ★ across to last 5 pegs, K5.

Row 2: Skip 1, K4, with CC K3, ★ with MC K1, with CC K3; repeat from ★ across to last 4 pegs, K4.

Row 3: Skip 1, P3, K1, with CC K3, ★ with MC K1, with CC K3; repeat from ★ across to last 4 pegs, P3, K1.

Row 4: Skip 1, P3, K2, with CC K1, ★ with MC K3, with CC K1; repeat from ★ across to last 5 pegs, K1, P3, K1.

Repeat Rows 1-4 for pattern until piece measures approximately 21" (53.5 cm) from cast on edge, ending by working Row 4; cut CC.

Work chain one bind off across *(Figs. 6a-c, page 60)* leaving a long end for sewing.

Weave bound off and cast on stitches together to form a circle *(Figs. 8b & c, page 61)*.

Knit & Purl Sampler

BEGINNER

Finished Size: 11" high x 32" circumference (28 cm x 81.5 cm)

SHOPPING LIST

Yarn (Medium Weight) MEDIUM 4

[3.5 ounces, 170 yards (100 grams, 156 meters) per skein]:

- ☐ Color A (Light Purple) - 1 skein
- ☐ Color C (Dark Purple) - 1 skein

[3 ounces, 145 yards (85 grams, 133 meters) per skein]:

- ☐ Color B (Print) - 1 skein

Loom (straight, large gauge)

- ☐ 50 Pegs

Additional Supplies

- ☐ Knitting loom tool
- ☐ Crochet hook, size K (6.5 mm)
- ☐ Yarn needle

GAUGE INFORMATION

In Stockinette Stitch (knit every row), 15 stitches and 20 rows = 4" (10 cm)

CHANGING COLORS

When changing colors, do **not** cut the yarn; drop the color that you are working with to the inside of the loom. Then pick up the next color from underneath the strand to twist the yarns *(Fig. 2, page 57)* and join the color sections together.

INSTRUCTIONS

This cowl is worked as flat knitting across the width. The ends will be sewn together to achieve the circumference.

Using Color A and working on the **inside** of the loom from right to left, chain cast on 15 pegs *(Figs. 1a & b, page 57)*, with Color B, chain cast on 11 pegs, with Color C, chain cast on 16 pegs; work as flat knitting: 42 pegs.

To skip 1 with yarn in back at the beginning of a row creates a finished look to the vertical edge. Place the working yarn **behind** the peg to be skipped.

Row 1: Skip 1, K3, (P3, K3) twice, with Color B K1, (P1, K1) 5 times, with Color A (K2, P4) twice, K3.

Row 2: Skip 1, K2, (P4, K2) twice, with Color B K1, (P1, K1) 5 times, with Color C knit across.

Row 3: Skip 1, P3, (K3, P3) twice, with Color B K11, with Color A P2, (K4, P2) twice, K1.

Row 4: Skip 1, P2, (K4, P2) twice, with Color B P11, with Color C knit across.

Row 5: Skip 1, K3, (P3, K3) twice, with Color B K1, (P1, K1) 5 times, with Color A P2, (K4, P2) twice, K1.

Row 6: Skip 1, P2, (K4, P2) twice, with Color B K1, (P1, K1) 5 times, with Color C knit across.

Row 7: Skip 1, P3, (K3, P3) twice, with Color B K11, with Color A P2, (K4, P2) twice, K1.

Row 8: Skip 1, P2, (K4, P2) twice, with Color B P11, with Color C knit across.

Repeat Rows 1-8 for pattern until piece measures approximately 32" (81.5 cm) from cast on edge, ending by working Row 8.

Work chain one bind off across ***(Figs. 6a-c, page 60)*** using matching color; cut yarns leaving long ends for sewing.

Weave bound off and cast on stitches together ***(Figs. 8b & c, page 61)***.

Mesh

Finished Size: 9" high x 33" circumference (23 cm x 84 cm)

SHOPPING LIST

Yarn (Medium Weight) MEDIUM 4
[3.5 ounces, 210 yards
(100 grams, 192 meters) per skein]:
☐ 1 skein

Loom (straight, large gauge)
☐ 50 Pegs

Additional Supplies
☐ Knitting loom tool
☐ Crochet hook, size K (6.5 mm)
☐ Yarn needle

GAUGE INFORMATION

In mesh pattern,
27 stitches = 7¾" (19.75 cm)

TECHNIQUES USED

Left decrease ***(Figs. 4a & b, page 58)***
Right decrease ***(Figs. 4d & e, page 59)***

INSTRUCTIONS

This cowl is worked as flat knitting across the width. The ends will be sewn together to achieve the circumference.

Working on the **inside** of the loom from right to left, chain cast on 32 pegs ***(Figs. 1a & b, page 57)***; work as flat knitting.

Row 1: Knit across.

To skip 1 with yarn in front before a decrease creates a hole. Move the loop from the peg to be skipped to the next peg, with yarn in **front** of the skipped peg, complete the decrease.

Row 2: K1, (skip 1 with yarn in **front**, right decrease) across to last 5 pegs, K5.

Row 3: Knit across.

Row 4: K1, (left decrease, skip 1 with yarn in **front**) across to last 5 pegs, P5.

Row 5: P5, knit across.

Repeat Rows 2-5 for mesh pattern until piece measures approximately 33" (84 cm) from cast on edge, ending by working Row 5.

Work sewn bind off across ***(Figs. 7a & b, page 60)*** leaving a long end for sewing.

Weave bound off and cast on stitches together ***(Figs. 8b & c, page 61)***.

Party

EASY +

Finished Size: 5" high x 32" circumference (12.5 cm x 81.5 cm)

SHOPPING LIST

Yarn (Fine Weight) 

[1.75 ounces, 202 yards
(50 grams, 185 meters) per skein]:

- ☐ Main Color - 1 skein

(Super Bulky Weight, Lace yarn) 

[27 yards (24 meters) per hank]:

- ☐ 1 hank

Loom (small gauge)

- ☐ 96 Pegs (minimum)

Additional Supplies

- ☐ Knitting loom tool
- ☐ Crochet hook, size H (5 mm)

This cowl is worked holding two strands of Main Color together as one throughout. Wind the yarn into two balls or pull one strand from the center and one from the outside of the skein.

GAUGE INFORMATION

In Twisted Garter Stitch (e-wrap knit 1 row, purl 1 row) and holding 2 strands of Main Color together,
12 stitches = 4" (10 cm),
18 rnds = 2¼" (5.75 cm)

INSTRUCTIONS

This cowl is worked as circular knitting beginning at the bottom ruffled edge.

The **right** side of the cowl is the side facing the inside of the loom.

RUFFLE

Work the cast on as follows: Bring Lace yarn up through the center of the loom and beginning with the first loop on edge of strand, place a loop on 96 pegs.

Rnds 1 and 2: ★ Place loop on peg, lift bottom loop over top loop and off peg; repeat from ★ around.

Cut Lace yarn close to work.

BODY

Rnd 1: Holding 2 strands of Main Color together, e-wrap knit around.

Rnd 2: Purl around.

Rnd 3: E-wrap knit around.

Rnds 4-17: Repeat Rnds 2 and 3, 7 times.

Rnd 18: Purl around.

Rnd 19: Knit around.

Rnds 20-26: Repeat Rnds 18 and 19, 3 times; then repeat Rnd 18 once **more**.

Work chain one bind off around *(Figs. 6a-c, page 60)*.

Ripple

Finished Size: 10" high x 40" circumference (25.5 cm x 101.5 cm)

SHOPPING LIST

Yarn (Medium Weight) MEDIUM 4
[3 ounces, 145 yards
(85 grams, 133 meters) per skein**]**:
- ☐ 2 skeins

Loom (straight, large gauge)
- ☐ 50 Pegs

Additional Supplies
- ☐ Knitting loom tool
- ☐ Crochet hook, size K (6.5 mm)
- ☐ Yarn needle

GAUGE INFORMATION

In pattern, 1 repeat (13 stitches) = 3¼" (8.25 cm)

INSTRUCTIONS

This cowl is worked as flat knitting across the width. The ends will be sewn together to achieve the circumference.

Working on the **inside** of the loom from right to left, chain cast on 41 pegs *(Figs. 1a & b, page 57)*; work as flat knitting.

Rows 1 and 2: Knit across.

Row 3 (Lace row)**:**
First, set up for the decreases beginning at the right edge. Move the loop from the 8th peg to the 9th peg, ★ skip next 11 pegs and move the loop from the next peg to the peg on the left; repeat from ★ once **more**.

Then, work the row beginning at the right edge. K2, ★ beginning with the peg before the empty peg, move the loops from the next 5 pegs one at a time to an empty peg, creating a different empty peg, skip 1 with yarn in **front**, K4, skip 1 with yarn in **back**, knit the next peg lifting the bottom 2 loops over the working yarn and off the peg. Move the loop just made to the skipped peg. Without knitting it, lift the bottom loop over the top loop and off the peg, move the loops from the next 4 pegs one at a time to the right, K4, skip 1 with yarn in **front**, K2; repeat from ★ across.

Row 4: P1, knit across to last peg, P1.

Row 5: Knit across.

Row 6: Purl across.

Repeat Rows 1-6 for pattern until piece measures approximately 40" (101.5 cm) from cast on edge, ending by working Row 2.

Work chain one bind off across *(Figs. 6a-c, page 60)* leaving a long end for sewing.

Weave bound off and cast on stitches together *(Figs. 8b & c, page 61)*.

Ruffled Chevron

INTERMEDIATE

Finished Size: 5" high x 28½" circumference (12.5 cm x 72.5 cm)

SHOPPING LIST

Yarn (Medium Weight) 

[3.5 ounces, 170 yards
(100 grams, 156 meters) per skein]:
- ☐ Main Color - 1 skein

(Super Bulky Weight, Fabric yarn) 

[30 yards (27 meters) per hank]:
- ☐ Contrasting Color - 1 hank

Loom (round, large gauge)
- ☐ 24 Pegs

Additional Supplies
- ☐ Knitting loom tool
- ☐ Crochet hook, size K (6.5 mm)
- ☐ Yarn needle

GAUGE INFORMATION

In Stockinette Stitch (knit every row), using Main Color,
14 stitches = 3¾" (9.5 cm),
1 repeat (26 rows) = 4¾" (12 cm)

WORKING WITH RUFFLE YARN

Only one peg on each row uses the Ruffle yarn (CC).

To purl 1 with Ruffle yarn, bring the Main Color (MC) to the inside of the loom, insert tool down through the loop on the peg (from top to bottom), using CC, pull next loop on CC up through loop on peg *(Fig. A)*.

Fig. A

Lift original loop off peg. Push CC between the cowl and the loom so that it will hang on the right side of the cowl when finished and place new CC loop onto empty peg. Move CC between the pegs to the outside of the loom and place MC behind peg just worked, then between the pegs to the outside of the loom ready to knit the next peg *(Fig. B)*.

Fig. B

INSTRUCTIONS

This cowl is worked as flat knitting across the width. The ends will be sewn together to achieve the circumference.

Working on the **inside** of the loom from right to left, and using MC, chain cast on 20 pegs *(Figs. 1a & b, page 57)*; work as flat knitting.

Row 1: P3, with CC P1, with MC K 13, P3.

Row 2: K 15, with CC P1, with MC K4.

Row 3: P3, K2, with CC P1, with MC K 11, P3.

Row 4: K 13, with CC P1, with MC K6.

Row 5: P3, K4, with CC P1, with MC K9, P3.

Row 6: K 11, with CC P1, with MC K8.

Row 7: P3, K6, with CC P1, with MC K7, P3.

Row 8: K9, with CC P1, with MC K 10.

Row 9: P3, K8, with CC P1, with MC K5, P3.

Row 10: K7, with CC P1, with MC K 12.

Row 11: P3, K 10, with CC P1, with MC K3, P3.

Row 12: K5, with CC P1, with MC K 14.

Row 13: P3, K 12, with CC P1, with MC K1, P3.

Row 14: K3, with CC P1, with MC K 16.

Row 15: P3, K 12, with CC P1, with MC K1, P3.

Row 16: K5, with CC P1, with MC K 14.

Row 17: P3, K 10, with CC P1, with MC K3, P3.

Row 18: K7, with CC P1, with MC K 12.

Row 19: P3, K8, with CC P1, with MC K5, P3.

Row 20: K9, with CC P1, with MC K 10.

Row 21: P3, K6, with CC P1, with MC K7, P3.

Row 22: K 11, with CC P1, with MC K8.

Row 23: P3, K4, with CC P1, with MC K9, P3.

Row 24: K 13, with CC P1, with MC K6.

Row 25: P3, K2, with CC P1, with MC K 11, P3.

Row 26: K 15, with CC P1, with MC K4.

Rows 27-156: Repeat Rows 1-26, 5 times; cut CC close to work.

Work chain one bind off across *(Figs. 6a-c, page 60)*.

Weave bound off and cast on stitches together *(Figs. 8b & c, page 61)*.

Scalloped Edge

EASY +

Shown on page 45.

Finished Size: 4½" high x 30" circumference (11.5 cm x 76 cm)

SHOPPING LIST

Yarn (Jumbo Weight) JUMBO 7
[5.29 ounces, 46 yards
(150 grams, 42 meters) per skein**]**:
☐ 1 skein

Loom (round, extra large gauge)
☐ 40 Pegs

Additional Supplies
☐ Knitting loom tool
☐ Crochet hook, size M/N (9 mm)

GAUGE INFORMATION

In Twisted Garter Stitch (e-wrap knit 1 row, purl 1 row),
4 stitches = 3" (7.5 cm)

INSTRUCTIONS

This cowl begins at the bottom edge with the scallops, then is worked as circular knitting.

SCALLOPED EDGE

Work scallops as follows:

Step 1: Working on the **inside** of the loom from right to left, chain cast on 5 pegs *(Figs. 1a & b, page 57)*.

Step 2: Without turning the loom and beginning with the first peg cast on (without working yarn attached), insert crochet hook in each loop (from bottom to top), removing them from the pegs *(Fig. A)*. *Note:* You can use your fingers or the tool to place the loops on the hook if it is easier.

Fig. A

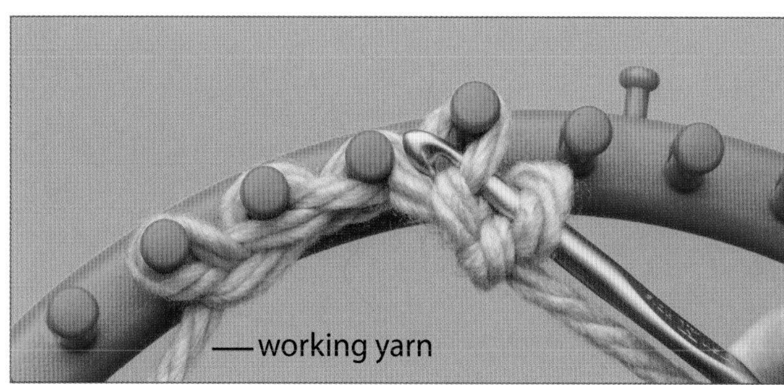

Step 3: Pull the last loop on the hook through remaining 4 loops to form a scallop *(Fig. B)*.

Fig. B

Step 4: Place loop onto first peg, with the scallop on the inside of the loom *(Fig. C)*, turn the loom and e-wrap next peg, e-wrap knit same peg.

Fig. C

Step 5: Working on the **inside** of the loom, place the e-wrapped stitch on the hook, keeping it tight *(Fig. D)*, chain cast on until there is a loop on 5 pegs from the scallop, place loop on hook on next empty peg: 6 pegs with loops after the last scallop made.

Fig. D

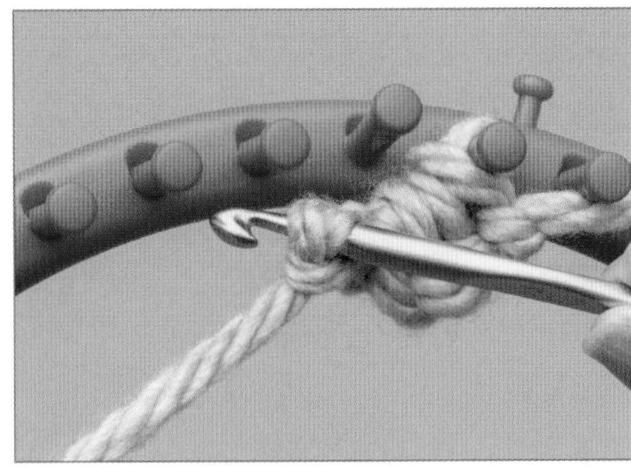

Step 6: Count back 5 pegs and being careful that the next loop stays on the peg, insert hook in each of the 5 loops, removing them from the pegs.

Step 7: Pull the last loop on the hook through remaining 4 loops.

Step 8: Place loop onto next empty peg with the scallop on the inside of the loom, turn the loom and e-wrap next peg, e-wrap knit same peg.

Repeat Steps 5-8 for each scallop for a total of 20 scallops and 20 e-wrap stitches. *Note:* There will not be enough empty pegs to work the last 2 scallops. Use the top of adjacent pegs to complete scallops.

BODY

Rnd 1: E-wrap knit around.

Rnd 2: Purl around.

Rnds 3-10: Repeat Rnds 1 and 2, 4 times.

Work chain one bind off around *(Figs. 6a-c, page 60)*.

Small Party

EASY +

Finished Size: 5½" high x 25" circumference at bottom edge of Body (14 cm x 63.5 cm)

SHOPPING LIST

Yarn (Medium Weight) MEDIUM 4
[3.5 ounces, 202 yards
(100 grams, 185 meters) per skein]:
- ☐ Main Color - 1 skein

(Super Bulky Weight, Lace yarn) SUPER BULKY 6
[27 yards (24 meters) per hank]:
- ☐ 1 hank

Loom (straight, large gauge)
- ☐ 50 Pegs

Additional Supplies
- ☐ Knitting loom tool
- ☐ Crochet hook, size K (6.5 mm)

This cowl is worked holding two strands of Main Color together as one throughout. Wind the yarn into two balls or pull one strand from the center and one from the outside of the skein.

GAUGE INFORMATION

In Twisted Garter Stitch (e-wrap knit 1 row, purl 1 row)
and holding 2 strands of Main Color together,
8 stitches = 4" (10 cm),
16 rnds = 3" (7.5 cm)

INSTRUCTIONS

This cowl is worked as circular knitting beginning at the bottom ruffled edge.

The **right** side of the cowl is the side facing the inside of the loom.

RUFFLE

Work the cast on as follows: Bring Lace yarn up through the center of the loom and beginning with the first loop on edge of strand, place a loop on all 50 pegs.

Rnds 1 and 2: ★ Place loop on peg, lift bottom loop over top loop and off peg; repeat from ★ around.

Cut Lace yarn close to work.

BODY

Rnd 1: Holding 2 strands of Main Color together, e-wrap knit around.

Rnd 2: Purl around.

Rnd 3: E-wrap knit around.

Rnds 4-15: Repeat Rnds 2 and 3, 6 times.

Rnd 16: Purl around.

Rnd 17: Knit around.

Rnds 18-24: Repeat Rnds 16 and 17, 3 times; then repeat Rnd 16 once **more**.

Work chain one bind off around ***(Figs. 6a-c, page 60)***.

Small Bandana

EASY

Finished Size: 8½" high x 22¼" circumference (21.5 cm x 56.5 cm)

SHOPPING LIST

Yarn (Bulky Weight) BULKY 5
[3.5 ounces, 148 yards
(100 grams, 136 meters) per skein]:
- ☐ 1 skein

Loom (straight, large gauge)
- ☐ 50 Pegs

Additional Supplies
- ☐ Knitting loom tool
- ☐ Crochet hook, size K (6.5 mm)
- ☐ Yarn needle

GAUGE INFORMATION

In Twisted Stockinette Stitch (e-wrap knit every row/rnd),
9 stitches and 18 rows/rnds = 4" (10 cm)

TECHNIQUES USED

- Left e-wrap decrease *(Fig. 4c, page 59)*
- Right e-wrap decrease *(Fig. 4f, page 59)*
- Left purl decrease *(Figs. 5a-c, page 59)*
- Right purl decrease *(Figs. 5d-f, page 59)*

INSTRUCTIONS

Working on the **inside** of the loom from right to left, chain cast on all 50 pegs *(Figs. 1a & b, page 57)*; work as circular knitting.

Rnd 1: E-wrap knit around.

Rnd 2: Purl around.

Rnds 3 and 4: Repeat Rnds 1 and 2.

Rnds 5-9: E-wrap knit around.

Rnd 10: P 14, EWK 22, P 14.

Rnd 11: E-wrap knit around.

Rnds 12 and 13: Repeat Rnds 10 and 11.

Rnd 14: Bind off 12 pegs using chain one bind off *(Figs. 6a & b, page 60)* and place loop from hook onto next empty peg, P2, EWK 22, P3; bind off last 11 pegs using chain one bind off, cut yarn and pull yarn end through loop *(Fig. 6c, page 60)*: 28 pegs remaining.

SHAPING

Row 1: Working from right to left, place a slip knot on an empty peg to temporarily hold the yarn in place; e-wrap knit across; remove slip knot.

When decreasing, move the end stitches so that there are no skipped pegs.

Row 2: P3, left e-wrap decrease, e-wrap knit across to last 5 pegs, right e-wrap decrease, P3: 26 pegs remaining.

Row 3: E-wrap knit across.

Rows 4-19: Repeat Rows 2 and 3, 8 times: 10 pegs remaining.

Row 20: P3, left e-wrap decrease, right e-wrap decrease, P3: 8 pegs remaining.

Row 21: E-wrap knit across.

Row 22: P2, left purl decrease, right purl decrease, P2: 6 pegs remaining.

Row 23: E-wrap knit across.

Row 24: P1, left purl decrease, right purl decrease, P1: 4 pegs remaining.

Row 25: E-wrap knit across.

Row 26: Left purl decrease, right purl decrease: 2 pegs remaining.

Row 27: EWK2.

Row 28: Left purl decrease; cut yarn and pull yarn end through loop.

Textured

EASY +

Finished Size: 6" high x 30" long unbuttoned (15.25 cm x 76 cm)

SHOPPING LIST

Yarn (Super Bulky Weight) 

[6 ounces, 106 yards
(170 grams, 97 meters) per skein]:
- ☐ 1 skein

Loom (round, large gauge)
- ☐ 24 Pegs

Additional Supplies
- ☐ Knitting loom tool
- ☐ Crochet hook, size K (6.5 mm)
- ☐ 1½" (38 mm) Buttons - 2
- ☐ Sewing needle and matching thread

GAUGE INFORMATION

In Seed Stitch, 13 stitches = 6" (15.25 cm)

TECHNIQUES USED

Left purl decrease *(Figs. 5a-c, page 59)*
Right purl decrease *(Figs. 5d-f, page 59)*

INSTRUCTIONS

This cowl is worked as flat knitting across the width. Buttons add style to the cowl.

BODY

Working on the **inside** of the loom from right to left, chain cast on 13 pegs *(Figs. 1a & b, page 57)*; work as flat knitting.

Row 1: (EWK1, P1) across to last peg, K1.

Row 2: P1, (EWK1, P1) across.

Repeat Rows 1 and 2 for Seed Stitch until piece measures approximately 28½" (72.5 cm) from cast on edge, ending by working Row 1.

Buttonhole Row: P1, EWK1, left purl decrease, skip 1 with yarn in **front** (buttonhole made), P1, (EWK1, P1) twice, move loop on next peg to next peg on the right, skip 1 with yarn in **front**, complete right purl decrease, EWK1, P1.

Repeat Rows 1 and 2, 4 times.

Work chain one bind off across *(Figs. 6a-c, page 60)*.

Using diagram as a guide for placement, sew 2 buttons to side edge of the opposite end of cowl to correspond with the buttonholes.

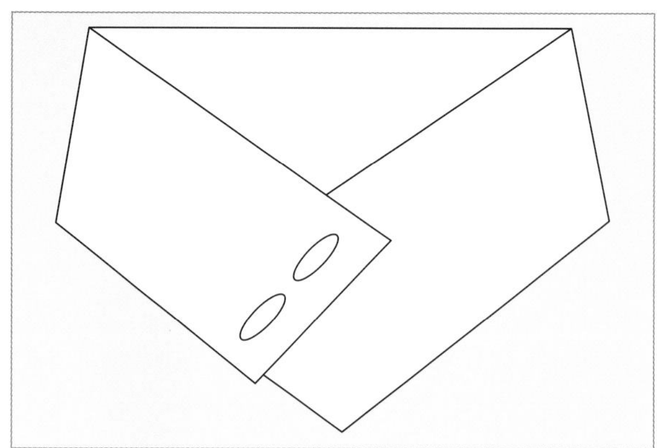

Twisted Ribs

INTERMEDIATE

Finished Size: 7" high x 24" circumference (18 cm x 61 cm)

SHOPPING LIST

Yarn (Medium Weight) 

[3.5 ounces, 170 yards
(100 grams, 156 meters) per skein]:
- ☐ 1 skein

Loom (straight, large gauge)
- ☐ 38 Pegs

Additional Supplies
- ☐ Knitting loom tool
- ☐ Crochet hook, size K (6.5 mm)
- ☐ Yarn needle

GAUGE INFORMATION

In Stockinette Stitch (knit every row),
15 stitches and 20 rows = 4" (10 cm)

STITCH GUIDE

LEFT TWIST (uses next 2 pegs)
Bring the working yarn to the inside of the loom, skip next peg (peg B), e-wrap next peg (peg A). Lift bottom loop over top loop and hold it on tool. Remove the loop from peg B with your fingers *(Fig. A)*, place the loop from the tool on peg B, then place loop you are holding on peg B. E-wrap knit peg B, bringing bottom 2 loops over top loop *(Fig. B)*. Skip peg A (already worked).

Fig. A

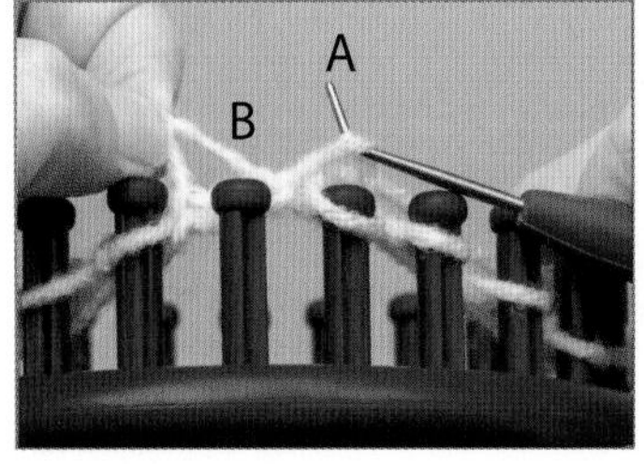

Fig. B

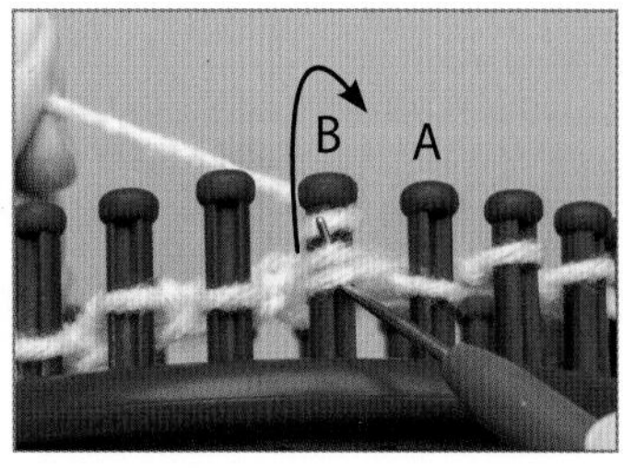

INSTRUCTIONS

This cowl is worked as flat knitting across the width. The ends will be sewn together to achieve the circumference.

Working on the **inside** of the loom from right to left, chain cast on 33 pegs *(Figs. 1a & b, page 57)*; work as flat knitting.

Row 1 AND ALL RIGHT TO LEFT ROWS: K1, (P1, K1) twice, P2, (K5, P2) 3 times, K1, (P1, K1) twice.

Row 2: (P1, K1) twice, P3, K3, Left Twist, ★ P2, K3, Left Twist; repeat from ★ once **more**, P3, (K1, P1) twice.

Row 4: (P1, K1) twice, P3, K2, Left Twist, K1, ★ P2, K2, Left Twist, K1; repeat from ★ once **more**, P3, (K1, P1) twice.

Row 6: (P1, K1) twice, P3, K1, Left Twist, K2, ★ P2, K1, Left Twist, K2; repeat from ★ once **more**, P3, (K1, P1) twice.

Row 8: (P1, K1) twice, P3, Left Twist, K3, ★ P2, Left Twist, K3; repeat from ★ once **more**, P3, (K1, P1) twice.

Repeat Rows 1-8 for pattern until piece measures approximately 24" (61 cm) from cast on edge, ending by working Row 8.

Work chain one bind off across *(Figs. 6a-c, page 60)*.

Weave bound off and cast on stitches together *(Figs. 8b & c, page 61)*.

Victorian Lace

INTERMEDIATE

Finished Size: 8" high x 19" circumference at top edge (20.5 cm x 48.5 cm)

SHOPPING LIST

Yarn (Bulky Weight) 

[3.5 ounces, 120 yards
(100 grams, 110 meters) per skein]:
- ☐ 1 skein

Loom (straight, large gauge)
- ☐ 38 Pegs

Additional Supplies
- ☐ Knitting loom tool
- ☐ Crochet hook, size K (6.5 mm)
- ☐ Yarn needle

GAUGE INFORMATION

In rib pattern,
14 stitches and 18 rows = 3¾" (9.5 cm)

TECHNIQUES USED

- Left decrease *(Figs. 4a & b, page 58)*
- Right decrease *(Figs. 4d & e, page 59)*

INSTRUCTIONS

This cowl is worked in two flat panels which are sewn together to achieve the circumference.

PANEL (Make 2)

Working on the **inside** of the loom from right to left, chain cast on 37 pegs *(Figs. 1a & b, page 57)*; work as flat knitting.

Row 1: ★ K3, P1, K2, P1; repeat from ★ across to last 2 pegs, K2.

Row 2: K2, ★ P1, right decrease, move stitch just made to empty peg, skip 1 with yarn in **front**, P1, K3; repeat from ★ across.

Row 3: ★ K3, P1, K2, P1; repeat from ★ across to last 2 pegs, K2.

Row 4: K2, ★ P1, skip next peg, move loop on next peg to skipped peg, then move both loops back to the empty peg, skip 1 with yarn in **front**, complete left decrease, P1, K3; repeat from ★ across.

Rows 5-20: Repeat Rows 1-4 (lace pattern), 4 times.

Row 21: ★ K3, P1, K2, P1; repeat from ★ across to last 2 pegs, K2.

Row 22: K2, ★ P1, K2, P1, K3; repeat from ★ across.

Repeat Rows 21 and 22 for rib pattern until piece measures approximately 8" (20.5 cm) from cast on edge, ending by working Row 21.

Work sewn bind off across *(Figs. 7a & b, page 60)*.

Matching bound off edges of Panels, weave end of rows together on each end to form the cowl *(Fig. 8a, page 61)*.

General Instructions

ABBREVIATIONS

CC	Contrasting Color
cm	centimeters
EWK	e-wrap knit
K	knit
MC	Main Color
mm	millimeters
P	purl
Rnd(s)	Round(s)

SYMBOLS & TERMS

★ — work instructions following ★ as many **more** times as indicated in addition to the first time.

( ) or **[ ]** — work enclosed instructions **as many** times as specified by the number immediately following **or** contains explanatory remarks.

colon (:) — the number(s) given after a colon at the end of a row or round denote(s) the number of of pegs you should have occupied at the end of that row or round.

working yarn — the strand coming from the skein.

GAUGE

Gauge is the number of stitches and rows or rounds in every inch of your knitting and is used to control the finished size.

Exact gauge is essential for proper size. Before beginning your project, make a sample swatch approximately 4" (10 cm) wide with the yarn and loom specified in the individual instructions. After completing the swatch, give it a tug, holding the cast on and bound off edges, then let it "rest."

Measure it, counting your stitches and rows carefully.

If your swatch is larger or smaller than specified, make another, changing your tension of the working yarn as you form the stitches. Keep trying until you find the tension you need to achieve gauge. Maintain established gauge throughout project.

Yarn Weight Symbol & Names	SUPER FINE 1	FINE 2	LIGHT 3	MEDIUM 4	BULKY 5	SUPER BULKY 6	JUMBO 7
Type of Yarns in Category	Sock, Fingering, Baby	Sport, Baby	DK, Light Worsted	Worsted, Afghan, Aran	Chunky, Craft, Rug	Bulky, Roving	Jumbo, Roving

BEGINNER	Projects for first-time loom knitters using basic knit and purl stitches, and simple color changes.
EASY	Projects using basic stitches, repetitive stitch patterns, simple color changes, and simple shaping and finishing.
EASY +	Projects using basic stitches, repetitive stitch patterns, simple color changes, simple short rows, and simple shaping and finishing.
INTERMEDIATE	Projects with a variety of stitches, such as lace, also short rows, and mid-level shaping and finishing.

CHAIN CAST ON

Leaving a 6" (15 cm) end, make a slip knot *(Figs. 9a-c, page 62)*, placing it on the crochet hook.

★ Working on the **inside** of the loom, you will cast on from **right** to **left**. Wrap the working yarn around the outside of the peg and bring it to the inside. Lay the working yarn on top of the crochet hook with the peg being encircled by the yarn. Catching the working yarn with the hook, bring it through the loop on the hook *(Fig. 1a)*, producing a chain stitch with the peg in the middle of the chain stitch.

Fig. 1a

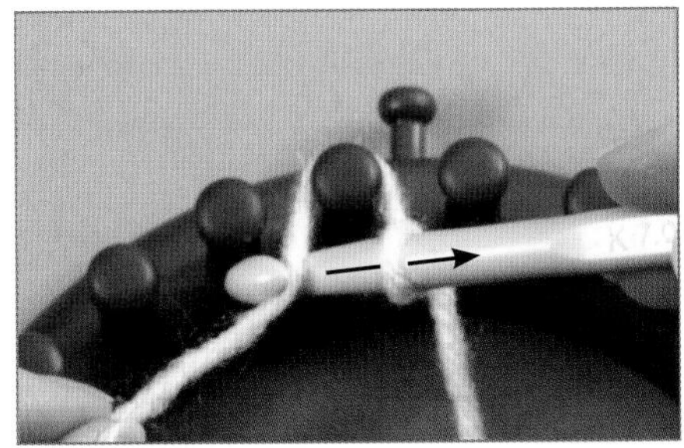

Repeat from ★ until you have cast on all but one peg needed.

For the last cast on stitch, keep the working yarn to the inside of the loom and place the loop from the hook onto the next empty peg *(Fig. 1b)*.

Fig. 1b

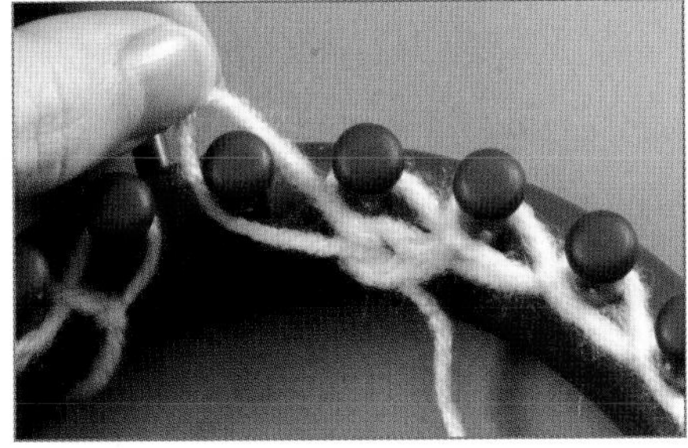

Turn the loom to work on the outside.

Note: To chain cast on working on the **outside** of the loom, hold the working yarn and crochet hook inside the loom. Work the same as before, only wrapping the yarn around the outside of the pegs *(Fig. 1c)*.

Fig. 1c

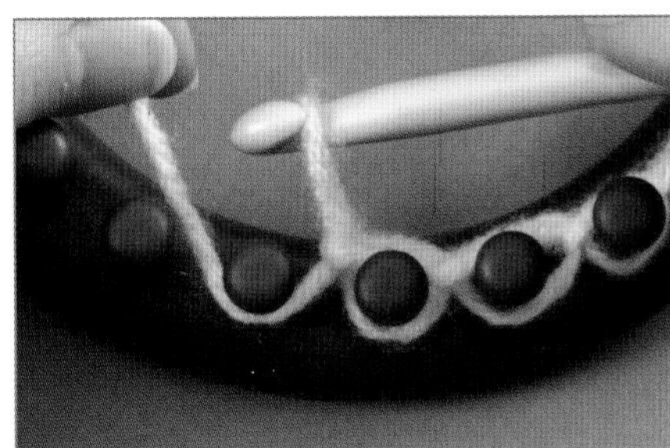

CHANGING COLORS

The first time the second color is used, drop the color that you are using to the inside of the loom and begin working with the new color leaving a long end to weave in later.

To change colors, drop the color that you are working with to the inside of the loom. Then pick up the next color from underneath the dropped strand *(Fig. 2)*. This will twist the yarns.

Do **not** cut the yarn unless specified.

Fig. 2

SHORT ROWS

Short rows are formed by only working across some of the pegs that have stitches on them before stopping and working back. This method adds extra length to some of the stitches for shaping such as on the Collared Lace (page 18) and the Hooded Cowl (page 28).

WRAPPING THE PEG

In order to prevent holes when working short rows, it is necessary to wrap the yarn around an unworked peg before changing directions.

Work across the pegs indicated in the pattern. Wrap the next peg as follows:

Step 1: Using the tool, lift the loop from the peg to be wrapped and hold it on the tool.

Step 2: Bring the working yarn behind the empty peg, then to the outside of the loom and across the front of the empty peg *(Fig. 3a)*. *Note:* Figs. show using double strands.

Fig. 3a

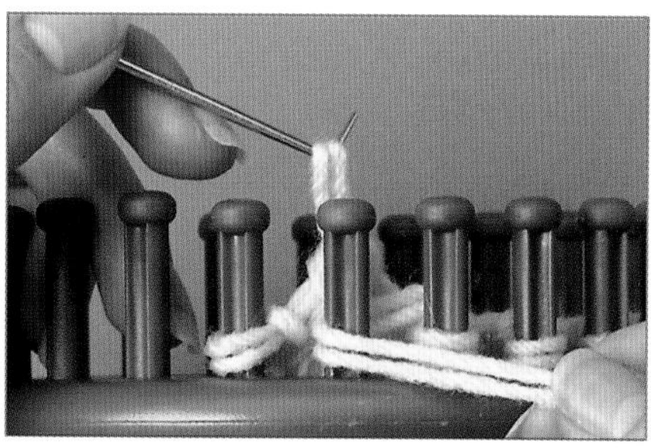

Step 3: Put the loop back onto the peg. The wrap will be under the loop *(Fig. 3b)*. Leave the remaining peg(s) unworked.

Fig. 3b

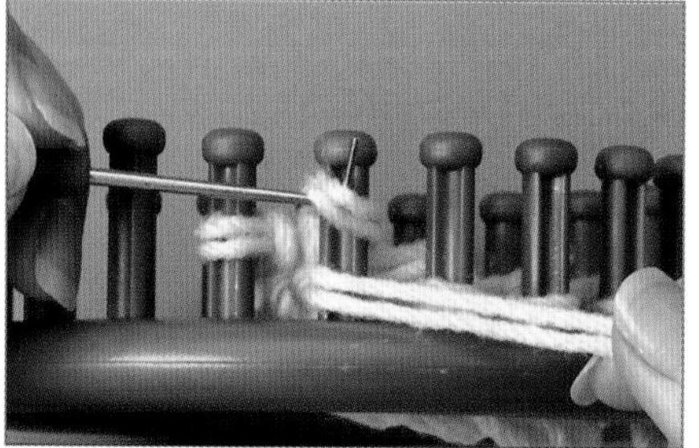

If you are working the e-wrap knit stitch method, bring the working yarn back to the inside of the loom so that it is in position to work back in the other direction.

DECREASES

All of the decreases are basically the same and it doesn't matter which direction the row or round is worked. A loop is moved to the peg next to it and then worked as one. What makes them different is which stitch is placed on top and whether the stitch is then knit, e-wrapped knit, or purled when worked together.

When decreasing the first or last stitch of a row for shaping, work the specified decrease. If it leaves an empty peg between the decrease and the work, move the new loop over to the empty peg.

LEFT DECREASE

Use the tool to move the loop from peg A to the **left** and place it on peg B, leaving peg A empty *(Fig. 4a)*.
Knit peg B, lifting the bottom 2 loops over the working yarn and off the peg *(Fig. 4b)*.

Fig. 4a

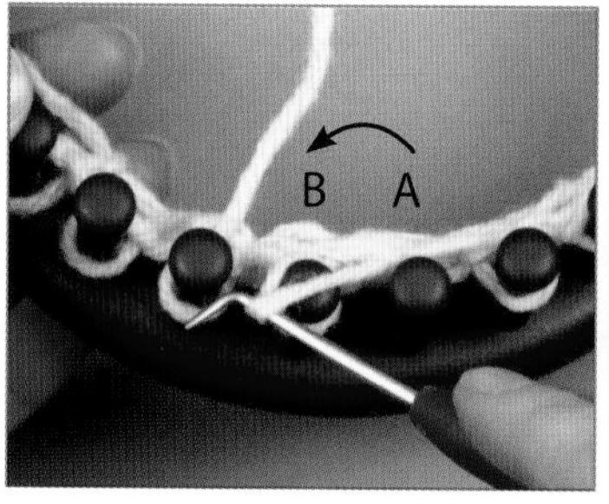

Fig. 4b

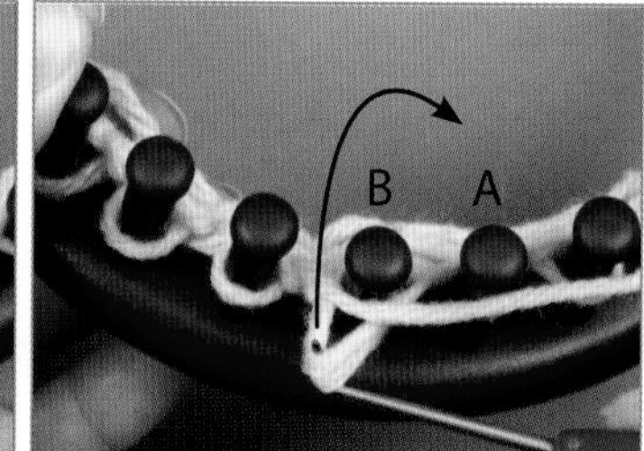

LEFT E-WRAP DECREASE

Use the tool to move the loop from peg A to the **left** and place it on peg B, leaving peg A empty *(Fig. 4a)*. E-wrap peg B *(Fig. 4c)* and lift the bottom 2 loops over the top loop and off the peg *(Fig. 4b)*.

Fig. 4c

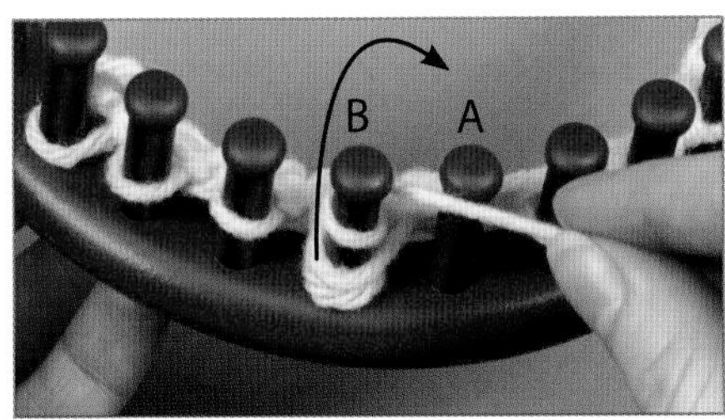

RIGHT DECREASE

Use the tool to move the loop from peg B to the **right** and place it on peg A, leaving peg B empty *(Fig. 4d)*. Knit peg A, lifting the bottom 2 loops over the working yarn and off the peg *(Fig. 4e)*.

Fig. 4d **Fig. 4e**

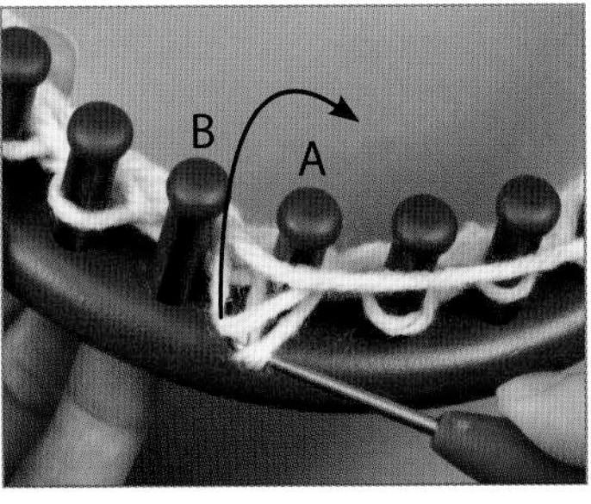

RIGHT E-WRAP DECREASE

Use the tool to move the loop from peg B to the **right** and place it on peg A, leaving peg B empty *(Fig. 4d)*. E-wrap peg A *(Fig. 4f)* and lift the bottom 2 loops over the top loop and off the peg *(Fig. 4e)*.

Fig. 4f

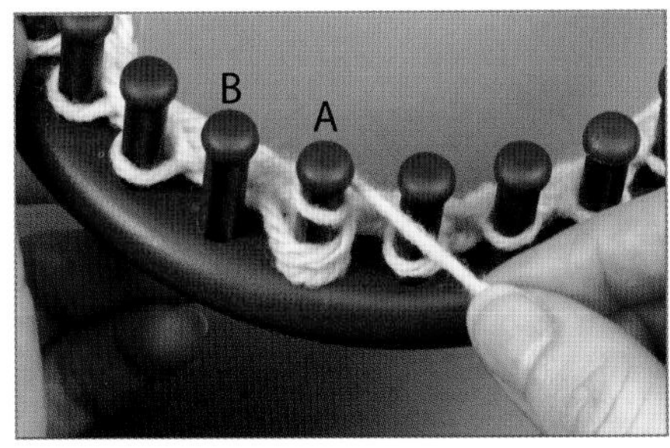

LEFT PURL DECREASE

Use the tool to move the loop from peg A to the **left** and place it on peg B, leaving peg A empty *(Fig. 5a)*.
Purl peg B working both strands as one *(Fig. 5b)*.

Fig. 5a **Fig. 5b**

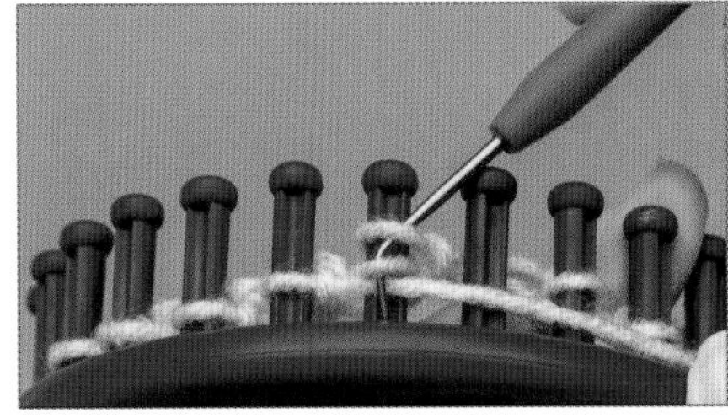

RIGHT PURL DECREASE

Use the tool to move the loop from peg B to the **right** and place it on peg A, leaving peg B empty *(Fig. 5c)*.
Purl peg A working both strands as one *(Fig. 5d)*.

Fig. 5c

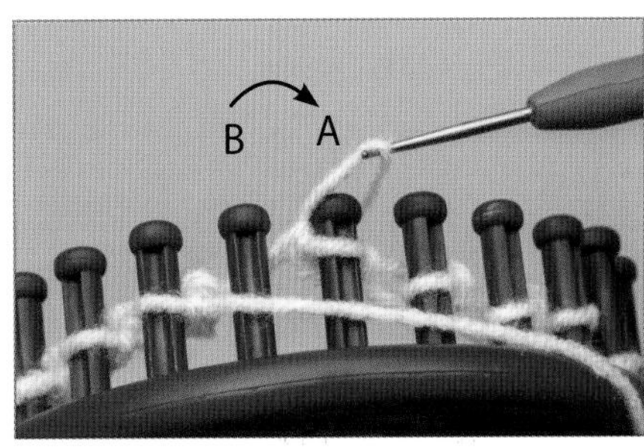

Fig. 5d

CHAIN ONE BIND OFF

With the working yarn to the inside of the loom, insert a crochet hook in the loop on the last peg worked, from **bottom** to **top**, and lift it off the peg. To chain 1, lay the working yarn on top of the crochet hook and bring it through the loop on the hook *(Fig. 6a)*, insert the hook in the loop on the next peg, from **bottom** to **top**, lift it off the peg and pull it through the loop on the hook *(Fig. 6b)*, ★ chain 1, insert the hook in the loop on the next peg, from **bottom** to **top**, lift it off the peg and pull it through the loop on the hook.

Fig. 6a

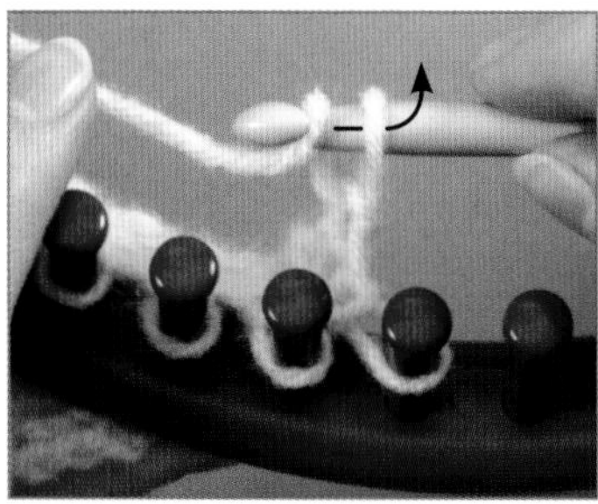

Fig. 6b

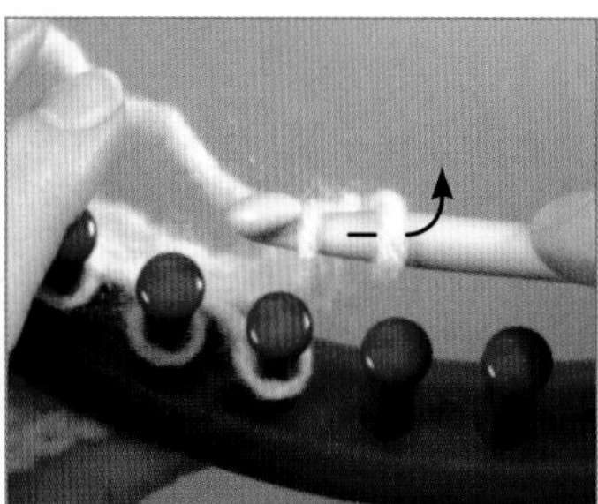

When binding off a certain number of stitches, repeat from ★ for each additional peg to be bound off. Bind off one extra peg and place the loop from the crochet hook back onto the empty peg unless otherwise instructed. Count the pegs remaining to be sure you have the correct amount.

When binding off all stitches, repeat from ★ until all of the loops have been removed from the loom and there is one loop left on the crochet hook. Chain 1, cut the yarn and pull the end through the final loop *(Fig. 6c)*; tighten the loop.

Fig. 6c

Note: If the last row was worked from right to left, you will need to hold the loom with the inner edge facing while binding off.

SEWN BIND OFF

Wrap the working yarn around the entire loom 3 times and cut the yarn at that point, giving you a long enough yarn to work the bind off. Unwrap the loom and thread the yarn needle with the end.

Step 1: Bring the yarn needle down through the loop on the first peg, then down through the loop on the second peg *(Fig. 7a)*.

Fig. 7a

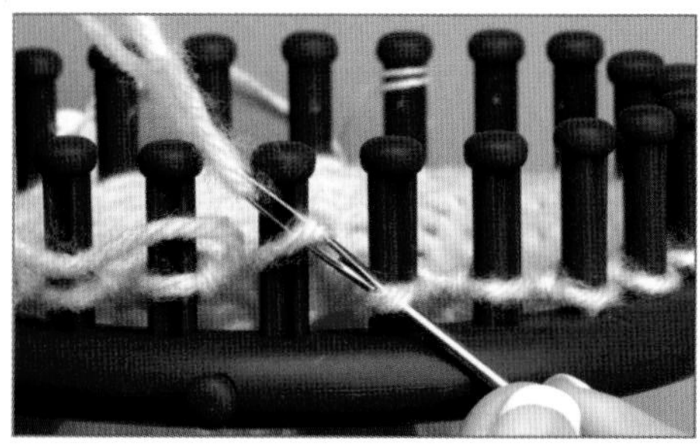

Step 2: Bring the yarn needle up through the loop on the first peg and lift it off the peg *(Fig. 7b)*, sliding it onto the yarn.

Fig. 7b

Repeat Steps 1 and 2 until one loop remains. Bring the yarn needle up through the loop on the remaining peg and lift it off the peg, pulling the yarn end through the loop.

WEAVING SEAMS

END OF ROWS

With the **right** side of both pieces facing you and edges even, sew through both sides once to secure the seam. Insert the needle under the bar between the first and second stitches on the row and pull the yarn through *(Fig. 8a)*. Insert the needle under the next bar on the second side. Repeat from side-to-side, being careful to match rows. If the edges are different lengths, it may be necessary to insert the needle under two bars at one edge.

Fig. 8a

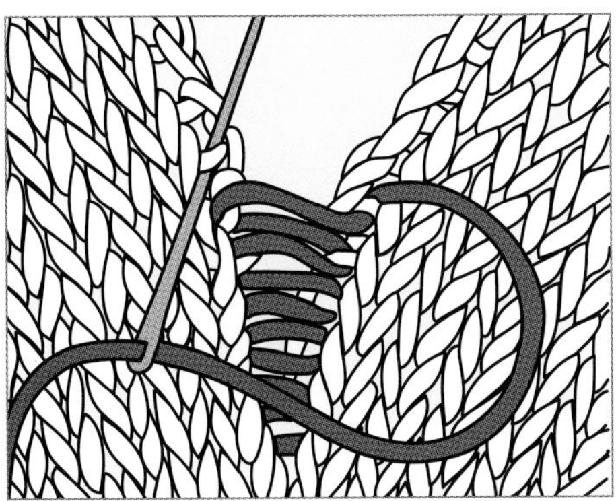

CAST ON & BOUND OFF EDGES

With the **right** side of both pieces facing you and matching edges, bring the yarn needle from behind the work and through the center of the first stitch. ★ Bring the yarn needle over the top of the edge and insert it under both loops of the corresponding stitch on the second side *(Fig. 8b)*. Bring the yarn needle back over the edge and insert it under the inverted V of the next stitch *(Fig. 8c)*. Repeat from ★ across. Pull the yarn gently every 2 or 3 stitches, being careful to maintain even tension.

Fig. 8b

Fig. 8c

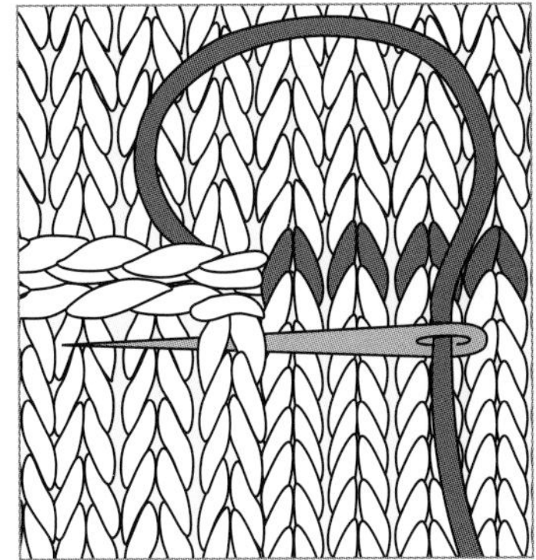

BASIC CROCHET STITCHES

SLIP KNOT

Make a circle and place the working yarn under the circle *(Fig. 9a)*. Either pick up the bar with your fingers and place it on the side peg of the loom, pulling both ends of the yarn to tighten the slip knot, **or** insert a crochet hook under the bar just made *(Fig. 9b)* and pull on both ends of the yarn to complete the slip knot forming a loop *(Fig. 9c)*.

Fig. 9a **Fig. 9b**

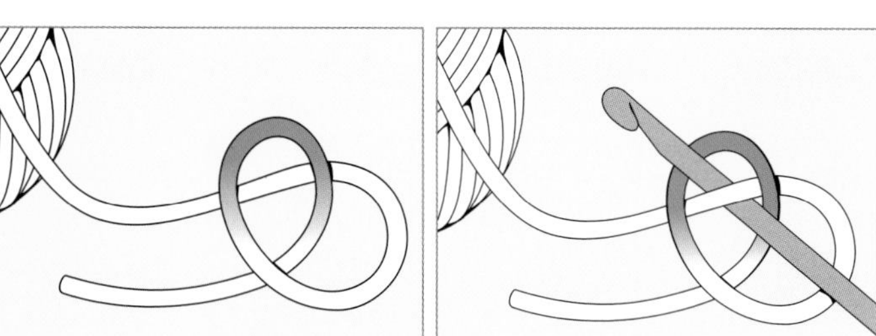

Fig. 9c

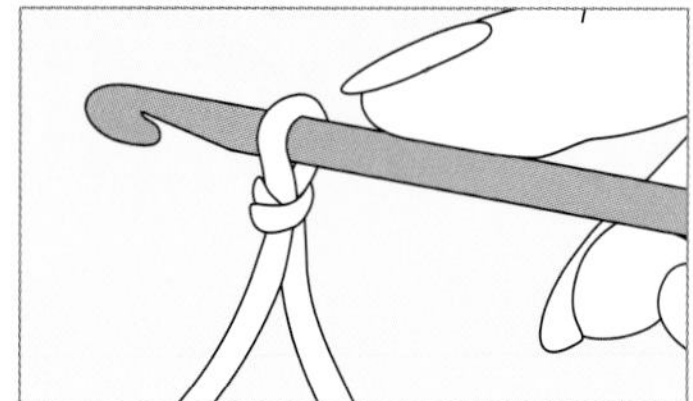

YARN OVER

Bring the yarn over the top of the hook from back to front, catching the yarn with the hook and turning the hook slightly toward you to keep the yarn from slipping off *(Fig. 10)*.

Fig. 10

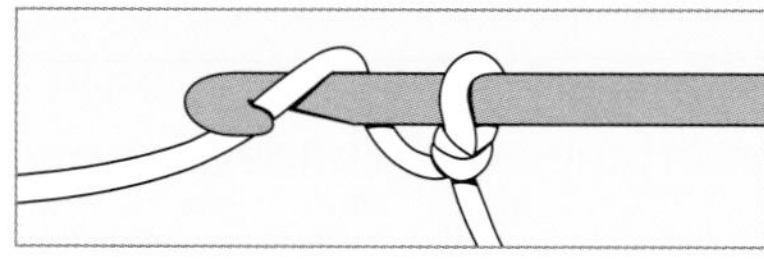

CHAIN

Yarn over *(Fig. 10)*, draw the yarn through the loop on the hook *(Fig. 11)*.

Fig. 11

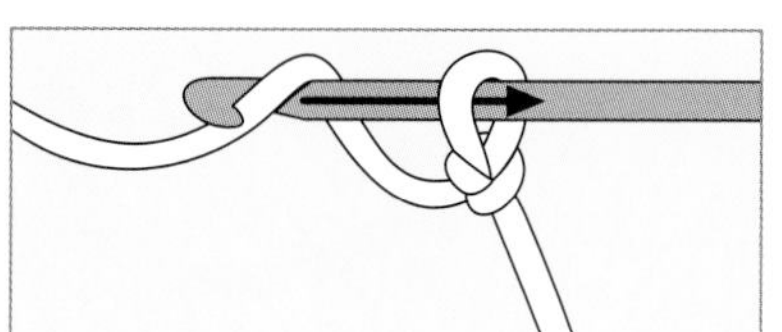

YARN INFORMATION

The cowls in this book were made using a variety of yarns. Any brand of the specified weight of yarn may be used. It is best to refer to the yardage/meters when determining how many skeins, balls, or hanks to purchase. Remember, to arrive at the finished size, it is the GAUGE/TENSION that is important, not the brand of yarn.

For your convenience, listed below are the yarns used to create our photography models. Because yarn manufacturers make frequent changes in their product lines, you may sometimes find it necessary to use a substitute yarn or to search for the discontinued product at alternate suppliers (locally or online).

ARGYLE
Patons® Canadiana™
Main Color (Green) - #10236 Medium Green Tea
Contrasting Color (Dark Green) - #10237 Dark Green Tea

BANDANA
Patons® Classic Wool DK Superwash™
#12008 Aran

BEEHIVE
Red Heart® Soft®
#9528 Lilac

BRIOCHE
Lion Brand® Heartland®
#135 Yosemite

BROKEN CABLES
Red Heart® Comfort® Chunky
#4456 Blue Jeans

CABLE LOOK-A-LIKE
Lion Brand® Wool-Ease® Thick & Quick®
#106 Sky Blue

COLLARED LACE
Patons® Decor™
#87430 Coral

DOUBLE RUFFLE
Bernat® Satin Sparkle™
Purple - #53307 Amethyst
Premier® Starbella® Flirt
Ruffle yarn - #5005 Canberra

MOBIUS
Red Heart® Boutique Treasure™
#1918 Abstract

FILIGREE
Premier® Deborah Norville Serenity® Chunky
White - #7020 Cloud Dancer
Black - #37 Raven

GATHERS
Lion Brand® Tweed Stripes®
#207 Rainforest

HOODED COWL
Bernat® Softee® Chunky™
#28425 Pale Antique Rose

HOUNDSTOOTH
Lion Brand® Heartland®
Main Color (Black) - #153 Black Canyon
Contrasting Color (Grey) - #151 Katmai

KNIT & PURL SAMPLER
Lion Brand® Vanna's Choice®
Color A (Light Purple) - #146 Dusty Purple
Color B (Print) - #303 Purple Mist
Color C (Dark Purple) - #147 Purple

MESH
Patons® Classic Wool Worsted™
#77208 Jade Heather

PARTY
Lion Brand® Vanna's Glamour®
Main Color - #114 Red Stone
Red Heart® Boutique Sassy Lace™
Lace yarn - #9902 Scarlet

RIPPLE
Lion Brand® Vanna's Tapestry
#204 Caribbean

RUFFLED CHEVRON
Lion Brand® Vanna's Choice®
Main Color - #123 Beige
Red Heart® Boutique Sassy Fabric™
Contrasting Color (Fabric yarn) - #9951 Tan Leopard

SCALLOPED EDGE
Red Heart® Grande™
#511 Wintergreen

SMALL PARTY
Red Heart® Boutique Swanky™
Main Color - #9522 Tealessence
Red Heart® Boutique Sassy Lace™
Lace yarn - #9501 Bora Bora

SMALL BANDANA
Patons® Shetland Chunky™
#78134 New Royal

TEXTURED
Lion Brand® Wool-Ease® Thick & Quick®
#138 Cranberry

TWISTED RIBS
Lion Brand® Vanna's Choice®
#105 Silver Blue

VICTORIAN LACE
Bernat® Alpaca™
#93420 Peony

Meet the Designer: Kathy Norris

Like most people, Kathy Norris learned to knit in the traditional style, using knitting needles. She discovered loom knitting at the craft supply store where she worked in Southern California. She says, "They handed me a knitting loom and told me to figure it out. So I taught myself how to use it."

Kathy used her first loom knitting designs to teach others the fun new skill. In 2005, she began publishing her patterns. "I was attracted to loom knitting because, as a designer, you have to find a new way to work with the geometry of knitting. Once you have the loom knitting basics down, you can start experimenting to make the loom do what you want."

For the cowls in this book, Kathy experimented with a wide variety of yarns and novelty materials to create lots of different looks and styles. Other Leisure Arts books featuring Kathy's designs are *More Knitting Wheel Fashions* (#4411), *I Can't Believe I'm Loom Knitting* (#5250), *Big Book of Loom Knitting* (#5604), *Loom Knitting for Mommy and Me* (#5942), *Loom Knit Hats and Scarves* (#75471) and *Loom Knit Dishcloths* (#6369). For more about Kathy, visit KathyNorrisDesigns.com.